INDIA'S SPIRITUAL LEGACY

DISCOVERING THE CULTURAL AND RELIGIOUS SIGNIFICANCE OF BHAKTI YOGA

DR. JAGADEESH PILLAI

|| Dedicated to all wisdom seekers around the World ||

ॐ

Contents

Contents

Prayer

**"Om Bhadram Karnebhih Shrunuyaama
DevaahBhadram Pashyemaakshabhiryajatraah
SthirairangaistushtuvaamsastanoobhihVyashema
Devahitam YadaayuhSwasti Na Indro
VridhashravaahSwasti Nah Pooshaa
VishwavedaahSwasti Nastaarkshyo ArishtanemihSwasti
No Brihaspatir DadhaatuOm Shantih, Shantih, Shantih"**

The literal meaning of this mantra is: OM. O Gods! Let us
hear auspicious words from our ears. O reverent Gods! Let
us behold propitious visions from our eyes, let our organs
and body be stable, healthy, and strong. Let us do that
which is pleasing to the gods in the life span allotted to us.
May Indra, inscribed in the scriptures, bring us fortune!
May Pushan, the knower of the world, grant us prosperity!
May Trakshya, who vanquishes enemies, bestow us with
blessings! May Brihaspati bring us success!
OM Peace, Peace, Peace.

About the Author

Dr. Jagadeesh Pillai is a renowned Guinness World Record holder, writer, and researcher hailing from Varanasi, also known as the abode of Lord Shiva. With a Ph.D. in Vedic Science and a range of creative ideas and achievements, he is a true polymath. He is the author of more than 100 books including Research Publications. Although his roots can be traced back to Kerala, the people of Varanasi hold him in high regard and affectionately consider him one of their own.

In 1998, Dr. Pillai was offered a job at Banaras Hindu University, but he left the position after only two months to pursue greater goals in life. He believed that in order to study Indian scriptures and engage in other creative endeavours, he needed to retire from the daily grind of working solely for money at a young age.

He started an export business from scratch, using the knowledge he had gained from a previous job in the industry. His intelligence and unique approach to business led to great success in a short period of time, earning him more in just a decade and a half than he would have in a lifetime working in a government job. Upon the passing of Dr. APJ Abdul Kalam, Dr. Pillai decided to leave the business and dedicate himself to reading, studying, researching, and experimenting.

During his tenure in the export business, Dr. Pillai traveled to over 16 countries, gaining valuable insight and experiencing the world and life in detail.

Dr. Pillai has achieved four Guinness World Records in the following subjects:

"Script to Screen" - In this record, Dr. Pillai produced and directed an animation film within the shortest time possible, breaking the previous record set by Canadians. He has also received numerous national and international awards and recognitions for this achievement.

Longest Line of Postcards - For this record, Dr. Pillai created a line of 16,300 postcards on the occasion of the 163rd anniversary of Indian Postal Day. The event also included a questionnaire about the Indian flag.

Largest Poster Awareness Campaign - Dr. Pillai designed an awareness campaign on the subject of "Beti Bachao - Beti Padhao" (Save the Girl Child - Educate the Girl Child) to achieve this record.

Largest Envelope - In tribute to the Indian Prime Minister's "Make in India" initiative, Dr. Pillai created a 4000 square meter envelope using waste paper to achieve this record.

Attempted - **70000 Candles on a 210 kg Cake** - To celebrate the 70th Indian Independence Day, Dr. Pillai attempted to light 70,000 candles on a 210 kg cake, which was recorded in World Records India.

Attempted - **Documentary on Dhamek Stupa of Sarnath in 17 Languages** - Dr. Pillai attempted to create a documentary on the Dhamek Stupa of Sarnath, dubbing it in 17 different languages. The result of this attempt is currently awaiting confirmation from the Guinness World Records.

Dr. Pillai is skilled in teaching the Bhagavad Gita, a Hindu scripture, and is popular among young people. He has helped many young people improve their lives through his motivational teachings.

In addition to teaching, he has composed and sung numerous Sanskrit Bhajans and patriotic songs.

He has also written and directed several short films and documentaries for awareness campaigns, and has volunteered with the police in both UP and Kerala to spread awareness about various issues through videos and photography.

Incredibly, he has produced and directed over 100 documentaries about the city of Varanasi, all on his own.

He has also helped and guided more than 25 boys and girls to achieve world records through creative and innovative methods. He is a multifaceted person who uses his intellect and the blessings given to him by God to excel in various areas. He is both a teacher and a student, always learning and teaching, and is able to master any subject he comes across.

He is a selfless social activist and motivational speaker who has overcome struggles and failures to become a successful and enthusiastic individual with a rich life experience.

In addition to his work with the Bhagavad Gita, he is also an efficient Tarot card reader, Astro-Vastu consultant, and a talented singer and composer. He has sung the entire Ram Charita Manas and Bhagavad Gita in his own compositions, and has sung the phrase "Lokah Samastha Sukhino Bhavantu" in 50 different languages. He is currently working on a detailed and scientific study of Vedas, Upanishads, Puranas, and the Bhagavad Gita. He has also composed and sung the Hanuman Chalisa and Gayatri Mantra in 108 and 1008 different compositions, respectively.

Awards - Four Times Guinness World Records, Winner of Mahatma Gandhi Vishwa Shanti Puraskar, Mahatma Gandhi Global Peace Ambassador, Kashi Ratna Award, Dr. APJ Abdul Kalam Motivational Person of the Year 2017, Mother Teresa Award, Indira Gandhi Priyadarshini Award, Bharat Vikas Ratna Award, Udyog Ratna Award, Vigyan Prasar Award, Poorvanchal Ratn Samman.

PREFACE

India is a land steeped in spirituality and cultural richness. Its ancient wisdom and spiritual traditions continue to influence and inspire people around the world to this day. One of the most significant and enduring of these spiritual traditions is Bhakti Yoga.

Bhakti Yoga is a path of devotion that has its roots in the ancient Vedic scriptures of India. It is a practice that is centered around the expression of love and devotion to a higher power, often embodied in the form of a deity. Over time, the Bhakti tradition has evolved to include a rich body of literature, music, and poetry that has inspired millions of people throughout history.

In this book, we aim to explore the cultural and religious significance of Bhakti Yoga in India and beyond. Through our journey, we will delve into the history of the Bhakti movement, examining its key figures, teachings, and practices. We will also explore the role of devotional music in Bhakti Yoga, as well as its practical applications in modern times.

Furthermore, we will examine the influence of Bhakti Yoga on spiritual traditions around the world, showcasing how this powerful and transformative path has impacted countless lives and inspired countless spiritual seekers.

Our aim in writing this book is to provide a comprehensive and in-depth exploration of the Bhakti tradition, offering a rich and nuanced understanding of its significance, both historically and in the present day. Whether you are a seasoned practitioner of Bhakti Yoga or simply someone who is curious about India's spiritual legacy, we believe that this book will be a valuable and enlightening resource.

I

Introduction to Bhakti Yoga: Understanding the Spiritual Roots of Bhakti

Bhakti Yoga is a spiritual path that has its roots in the ancient cultural and religious traditions of India. It is a form of yoga that is centered around the devotion to a personal deity or to the divine in general. Bhakti Yoga is one of the most popular spiritual paths in India, and it continues to be an important part of the country's spiritual heritage.

Bhakti Yoga emphasizes the importance of a personal relationship with the divine, and it is seen as a way to purify the mind and heart, and to deepen one's spiritual connection with the divine. It is believed that through the practice of Bhakti Yoga, one can attain inner peace and happiness, and that one can become closer to the divine.

The origins of Bhakti Yoga can be traced back to the ancient scriptures of India, such as the Vedas and the Puranas. Bhakti Yoga is often associated with the Bhagavad Gita, a Hindu scripture that is considered to be one of the most important spiritual texts in India. The Bhagavad Gita provides a comprehensive guide to Bhakti Yoga, and it lays out the principles and practices of this spiritual path.

Bhakti Yoga is characterized by its focus on devotion, and it is seen as a path to enlightenment that is open to all, regardless of one's background or social status. It is a path that requires no special knowledge or training, and it can be practiced by anyone who is willing to dedicate their heart and mind to the divine.

In Bhakti Yoga, the devotee is encouraged to express their love and devotion to the divine through various means, such as singing, praying, and offering gifts. The practice of Bhakti Yoga requires a deep level of commitment and devotion, and it requires the devotee to surrender their ego and their desires to the divine.

Bhakti Yoga is a spiritual path that is centered around the devotion to the divine. It is a path that emphasizes the importance of a personal relationship with the divine, and it is seen as a way to attain inner peace and happiness. Bhakti Yoga is an important part of India's spiritual heritage, and it continues to be a popular spiritual path in India today. Through the practice of Bhakti Yoga, individuals can deepen their spiritual connection with the divine, and they can become closer to the divine.

"India's spiritual legacy is a rich tapestry of diverse beliefs, practices and traditions that have shaped the country's cultural and religious landscape for thousands of years."

‿

II

The Bhakti Movement in Medieval India: A Historical Perspective

The Bhakti Movement was a significant religious and cultural movement in medieval India, which had a profound impact on Indian society and spirituality. This movement marked a significant shift in the religious landscape of India, as it emphasized the importance of devotion and personal relationship with the divine, as opposed to the more philosophical and ritualistic practices that dominated the religious scene at the time.

The Bhakti Movement emerged in the early medieval

period, between the 7th and the 13th centuries. It was a response to the increasing influence of Buddhism and Jainism, which threatened the dominance of Hinduism in India. The Bhakti Movement aimed to revitalize Hinduism and to make it more accessible to the masses.

One of the key figures of the Bhakti Movement was the philosopher and poet, Shankara. Shankara was a strong advocate of the Bhakti path, and his works helped to spread the message of Bhakti Yoga to a wider audience. He emphasized the importance of devotion, love, and surrender to the divine, and his teachings inspired many to embrace Bhakti Yoga as a way of life.

Another important figure of the Bhakti Movement was the saint, Ramanuja. Ramanuja was a philosopher and theologian who played a significant role in spreading the message of Bhakti Yoga. He emphasized the importance of devotion and the role of the devotee in attaining spiritual liberation. His teachings were highly influential, and they helped to shape the Bhakti Movement and to make it more accessible to the masses.

The Bhakti Movement was characterized by its emphasis on devotion and personal relationship with the divine, as opposed to the more philosophical and ritualistic practices of the time. The movement encouraged the expression of devotion through singing, dancing, and other forms of devotional practices. It also emphasized the importance of community, and it encouraged people to come together to practice Bhakti Yoga and to support one another on their spiritual journey.

The Bhakti Movement had a profound impact on Indian society and spirituality. It revitalized Hinduism and made it more accessible to the masses. It also helped to shape the religious and cultural landscape of India, and it continues to be an important part of India's spiritual heritage to this day.

The Bhakti Movement was a significant religious and cultural movement in medieval India, which had a profound impact on Indian society and spirituality. It marked a significant shift in the religious landscape of India, as it emphasized the importance of devotion and personal relationship with the divine, and it revitalized Hinduism and made it more accessible to the masses. The Bhakti Movement continues to be an important part of India's spiritual heritage to this day, and it continues to inspire people to embrace Bhakti Yoga as a way of life.

"The Bhakti movement, a central aspect of
India's spiritual legacy, is a devotional
tradition that emphasizes the love and
devotion towards a personal deity."

☙

III

Exploring Bhakti Literature: From the Bhagavad Gita to Bhakti Poetry and Hymn

The Bhakti movement in medieval India gave rise to a rich tradition of literature that expressed devotion to a personal deity. This literature played an important role in shaping the religious and cultural landscape of India, and it continues to inspire people to this day. From devotional hymns and poems to ancient scriptures and commentaries, Bhakti literature encompasses a wide range of works that reflect the diverse experiences and beliefs of India's Bhakti yogis.

One of the most well-known and influential works of Bhakti literature is the Bhagavad Gita. This ancient Hindu scripture is a part of the larger epic, the Mahabharata, and is considered one of the most important spiritual texts in Hinduism. The Bhagavad Gita is a dialogue between the prince Arjuna and the god Krishna, in which Krishna offers Arjuna guidance and wisdom on the nature of reality and the path to enlightenment. The text is often studied as a guide to Bhakti yoga, as it stresses the importance of devotion and surrender to the divine as a means of attaining liberation.

In addition to the Bhagavad Gita, the Bhakti movement gave rise to a large body of devotional poetry and hymns. These works were often composed in regional languages, such as Sanskrit, Tamil, and Hindi, and were sung in the temples and at festivals. They often contained stories and songs that celebrated the devotion and love of the Bhakti yogis for their chosen deity, and served as a means of transmitting the teachings of the Bhakti movement to the masses.

Bhakti poetry and hymns were often composed by saints and mystics who were inspired by their personal experiences of the divine. Some of the most famous Bhakti saints include Kabir, Mirabai, and Tulsidas, who expressed their devotion through their poetry and hymns. These works often contained imagery and symbolism that reflected the Bhakti yogi's relationship with their chosen deity, and they provided a way for people to connect with the divine through their devotion.

Another important aspect of Bhakti literature is the tradition of devotional songs, or bhajans. These songs were often sung in the temples and at festivals, and they served as a means of expressing devotion and connecting with the divine. Bhajans often contained lyrics that praised the chosen deity and expressed the Bhakti yogi's love and devotion for their chosen deity. These songs were often accompanied by musical instruments, such as the harmonium and the tabla, and they provided a way for people to connect with the divine through their musical and spiritual practice.

Bhakti literature plays an important role in the spiritual and cultural heritage of India. From ancient scriptures and commentaries to devotional hymns and poems, these works provide a window into the beliefs and practices of the Bhakti movement, and they continue to inspire people to this day. Whether one is seeking to deepen their spiritual understanding or simply to appreciate the rich cultural heritage of India, Bhakti literature provides a valuable resource for exploration and discovery.

"The Bhakti tradition has had a profound influence on Indian society and has left a lasting impact on the country's spiritual and cultural heritage.

୧

IV
The Saints of Bhakti movement: The Lives and Teachings of great Bhakti saints like Kabir, Meera, Ravidas, Tukaram and more

The Bhakti movement, which originated in India in the medieval period, has produced a number of great saints and spiritual leaders who have left an indelible mark on Indian religious and cultural history. These saints, through their lives and teachings, embody the essence of Bhakti yoga and its principles of devotion, love, and surrender to a higher power. In this chapter, we will explore the lives and teachings of some of the most revered Bhakti saints, including Kabir, Meera, Ravidas, Tukaram, and others.

Kabir

Kabir was a 15th century Indian mystic poet and saint who is considered to be one of the greatest saints of the Bhakti movement. Born in the city of Varanasi, Kabir lived a simple life and was known for his devotion to God and his criticism of religious rituals and dogmas. He was a strong advocate of the idea that true spirituality lies in a direct, personal relationship with God, and not in external religious practices. His poems, which are characterized by their simple yet powerful language, have been widely popular and continue to be recited and sung to this day.

Meera

Meera, also known as Mirabai, was a 16th century princess who became a great devotee of Lord Krishna. Born into a royal family, Meera's devotion to Krishna was so strong that she rejected her royal duties and dedicated her life to serving God. She is famous for her devotional songs and hymns, which are considered to be among the greatest expressions of Bhakti. Meera's life and teachings demonstrate the depth of love and devotion that can be attained through Bhakti yoga, and she remains an inspiration to millions of people today.

Ravidas

Ravidas was a 15th century saint and poet who lived in northern India. He was a leather worker by profession and is considered to be one of the greatest saints of the Bhakti movement. Ravidas was a strong advocate of the idea that God is present in all beings, regardless of their social status or caste, and that true devotion requires the recognition of this divine presence in others. His teachings emphasize the importance of compassion and selflessness, and his poems and hymns continue to be popular among devotees of Bhakti yoga.

Tukaram

Tukaram was a 17th century saint and poet who lived in the western Indian state of Maharashtra. He is considered to be one of the greatest saints of the Bhakti movement and is revered by millions of devotees across India. Tukaram's poems, which are characterized by their simple language and powerful expression of devotion, are considered to be some of the greatest works of Bhakti literature. Through his life and teachings, Tukaram demonstrated the power of Bhakti yoga to bring about transformation and enlightenment.

The Bhakti movement has produced a number of great saints and spiritual leaders who have left an indelible mark on Indian religious and cultural history. Their lives and teachings embody the essence of Bhakti yoga and continue to inspire millions of people today. Through their devotion, love, and surrender to a higher power, these saints demonstrate the power of Bhakti to bring about personal transformation and spiritual enlightenment.

ॐ

"The saints of the Bhakti movement, such as Kabir, Meera, Ravidas, and Tukaram, have inspired generations with their teachings of love, devotion, and equality."

৪৩

V

The Bhakti tradition in different Indian Languages: the Poetry and Hymns of the Bhakti Saints in Different Languages

The Bhakti tradition in different Indian languages is a testament to the widespread influence of the Bhakti movement in medieval India. The Bhakti saints and their teachings were not limited to one particular language or region, but instead spread throughout the country, reaching people from all walks of life.

In northern India, the Bhakti saints wrote and sang in Hindi, Punjabi, and Braj Bhasha, the local language of the region. Kabir, one of the most famous Bhakti saints, wrote poetry and hymns in Hindi that reflected his beliefs and teachings. His poetry, which was simple and direct, spoke of the importance of devotion to God and the ultimate unity of all religions.

In western India, the Bhakti saints wrote and sang in Marathi, a regional language that was widely spoken in the area. Tukaram, a prominent Bhakti saint of this region, wrote devotional poetry in Marathi that was characterized by its simplicity and emotional intensity. His poems spoke of his love for God and his deep devotion to the divine.

In southern India, the Bhakti saints wrote and sang in Tamil and other regional languages. The poems and hymns of the Bhakti saints in this region were characterized by their devotional themes, as well as their use of vivid imagery and symbolism. One of the most famous Bhakti saints in this region was Andal, who wrote devotional poetry in Tamil that was celebrated for its beauty and devotion.

The Bhakti tradition in different Indian languages is a rich and diverse expression of the Bhakti movement. The poems and hymns of the Bhakti saints, written in different languages and regions, reflect the spiritual and cultural diversity of India and its people. The Bhakti tradition in different Indian languages is not only a testament to the influence of the Bhakti movement, but also to the enduring power of devotion and spirituality in Indian culture.

"The poetry and hymns of the Bhakti saints, written in different languages, have become an integral part of India's cultural and spiritual legacy."

ॐ

VI

The Bhakti tradition in different regions of India: Regional Variations of Bhakti Yoga and Practices

The Bhakti tradition, which is centered around the devotion to a personal god, has been a defining characteristic of Indian spirituality for centuries. While Bhakti Yoga has its roots in the ancient scriptures, it has evolved and adapted over time, taking on unique forms and expressions in different regions of India. In this chapter, we will explore the regional variations of Bhakti Yoga and the unique practices that have emerged in different parts of the country.

South India: Bhakti in South India has been shaped by the Vaishnavite and Shaivite traditions, which are centered around the devotion to Lord Vishnu and Lord Shiva, respectively. The Bhakti movement in South India reached its peak in the 8th century, with the rise of the Alvar and Nayanar saints, who composed hymns in the local languages of Tamil and Sanskrit, which are still revered by devotees today.

One of the most notable examples of Bhakti in South India is the Bhagavata Mela, a dance-drama performance that re-enacts the life of Lord Krishna and is held annually in the state of Tamil Nadu. Another popular practice in South India is the recitation of the "Stotras," which are hymns of praise to the deity, and the singing of "Bhajans," which are devotional songs.

North India: In North India, the Bhakti movement was heavily influenced by the teachings of the saints Kabir, Ravidas, and Meera, who advocated for the equality of all beings and the importance of devotion to a personal god. This emphasis on devotion has led to the creation of a rich tradition of Bhakti poetry and hymns, including the "Padavali" genre of devotional poetry, which is widely popular in North India.

In North India, the Bhakti movement is also closely tied to the Sufi tradition, which emphasizes the importance of love and devotion in reaching a higher state of consciousness. This has led to the creation of unique forms of Bhakti yoga, such as the "Qawwali," which is a form of devotional music that combines elements of Bhakti and Sufi spirituality.

West India: In West India, Bhakti Yoga has been heavily influenced by the teachings of the saint Tukaram, who was a prominent figure in the Bhakti movement in the 17th century. Tukaram's poetry and hymns, which were written in the Marathi language, emphasize the importance of devotion to a personal god and the role of devotion in attaining a higher state of consciousness.

In West India, Bhakti Yoga is also closely tied to the tradition of "Dindi," which is a form of devotional singing and dancing that is performed by devotees during religious festivals. This practice has become a central part of the Bhakti tradition in West India and is a way for devotees to express their love and devotion to a personal god.

East India: In East India, Bhakti Yoga has been shaped by the teachings of the saint Chaitanya, who was a prominent figure in the Bhakti movement in the 16th century. Chaitanya's teachings emphasized the importance of devotion to a personal god and the role of devotion in attaining a higher state of consciousness.

In East India, Bhakti Yoga is closely intertwined with the ancient tradition of Kirtan, a form of devotional singing and chanting that is performed by devotees during religious festivals. This practice has become a cornerstone of spiritual practice in the region, providing a powerful way for devotees to express their devotion to the divine. Kirtan is often accompanied by traditional instruments such as the harmonium, tabla, and mridangam, and is often accompanied by ecstatic dancing and clapping. Through Kirtan, devotees can experience a deep connection to the divine, and can find a sense of peace and joy.

The Bhakti tradition in India has a rich and diverse history, with variations emerging in different regions of the country. These regional variations are influenced by the local culture, language, and religious practices, making each region's interpretation of Bhakti unique.

For example, the Bhakti tradition in South India, known as the "Bhakti Movement of South India", was heavily influenced by the Vaishnavite tradition and was marked by the devotion to Lord Vishnu. This movement saw the rise of great saints like Andal, Ramanuja, and Nammalvar, who propagated the teachings of Bhakti through their poetry and hymns. The compositions of these saints are considered to be some of the most important works of Bhakti literature, and continue to be widely studied and revered today.

In contrast, the Bhakti tradition in the northern regions of India was marked by the devotion to Lord Shiva, with saints like Kabir, Ravidas, and Tukaram propagating the teachings of Bhakti through their hymns and poems. These saints, who hailed from diverse backgrounds, including Hinduism, Islam, and Sikhism, were known for their inclusive and universal approach to spirituality, and their teachings continue to be a source of inspiration for people across India and beyond.

In the western region of India, the Bhakti tradition was marked by the devotion to Lord Krishna, and saw the rise of great saints like Meera, Surdas, and Chaitanya Mahaprabhu. These saints propagated the teachings of Bhakti through their devotional songs and poems, and their works continue to be widely studied and revered today.

The Bhakti tradition in India is rich and diverse, with regional variations that reflect the cultural, linguistic, and religious influences of each region. Whether it is the Vaishnavite tradition in South India, the devotion to Lord Shiva in the north, or the devotion to Lord Krishna in the west, the Bhakti tradition remains a central part of India's spiritual heritage, and continues to be an important source of inspiration and guidance for people all over the world.

"Music has played a central role in the Bhakti tradition, serving as a powerful tool for devotional expression and connecting with the divine."

৪৩

VII

The Bhakti tradition in relation to other forms of Yoga: Comparison with Jnana and Karma Yoga

The Bhakti tradition, although one of the most prominent spiritual practices in India, is not the only form of yoga present in the country. There are two other forms of yoga that have been widely practiced in India: Jnana Yoga and Karma Yoga. It is important to understand the relationship between Bhakti Yoga and these other forms of yoga, as they all have their own unique perspectives and approaches to spiritual development.

Jnana Yoga, also known as the path of knowledge, is focused on gaining knowledge of the self and the ultimate reality through introspection, self-reflection, and philosophical inquiry. Jnana Yoga emphasizes the use of the intellect and reasoning to attain enlightenment. It holds that the path to ultimate liberation lies in realizing the true nature of reality, and that the individual self and the ultimate reality are one and the same.

Karma Yoga, on the other hand, is the path of action. It emphasizes the importance of performing actions that are selfless and detached, with the ultimate goal of purifying the mind and realizing the ultimate reality. Karma Yoga holds that one's actions are the most important aspect of spiritual development, and that performing actions with a pure and selfless motivation can lead to spiritual liberation.

Bhakti Yoga, in comparison, is the path of devotion. It is focused on the development of a personal relationship with the divine, through practices such as devotion, worship, and prayer. Bhakti Yoga holds that the path to ultimate liberation lies in developing a deep and intimate connection with the divine, and that this connection can be cultivated through devotion and love.

It is important to note that these three forms of yoga are not necessarily mutually exclusive, and many practitioners may incorporate elements of all three into their spiritual practice. Additionally, each form of yoga has its own unique strengths and weaknesses, and individuals may find that one form of yoga is more suited to their individual needs and perspectives.

The Bhakti tradition, although distinct from Jnana and Karma Yoga, is closely related to these other forms of yoga. By understanding the relationship between Bhakti Yoga and these other forms of yoga, we can gain a deeper appreciation for the diverse spiritual practices that exist in India, and for the rich cultural and spiritual heritage of the country.

"Bhakti yoga, as a form of yoga, offers a path towards self-realization and spiritual growth through devotion and love."

VIII

Bhakti in Modern India: The contemporary resurgence of Bhakti Yoga and its Impact

The Bhakti tradition has been an integral part of India's spiritual and cultural heritage for many centuries. In recent times, however, Bhakti Yoga has experienced a resurgence in popularity, as people seek a return to the country's spiritual roots and a greater connection with the divine. In this chapter, we will explore the contemporary resurgence of Bhakti Yoga and its impact on modern India.

One of the main factors contributing to the resurgence of Bhakti Yoga is the growing interest in spirituality and mindfulness in our fast-paced, technology-driven world. People are seeking ways to slow down, connect with their inner selves, and find peace in their lives. Bhakti Yoga offers a way for people to connect with the divine and experience a sense of inner peace, regardless of their religious or spiritual background.

Another factor contributing to the resurgence of Bhakti Yoga is the growing popularity of yoga and meditation in the West. As more people learn about the benefits of yoga and meditation, they are seeking out spiritual practices that have roots in India's rich spiritual heritage. Bhakti Yoga is one such practice, offering a way for people to connect with the divine through devotional practices, such as singing, chanting, and prayer.

The contemporary resurgence of Bhakti Yoga has also been helped along by the increasing availability of resources, including books, CDs, and online content. This has made it easier for people to learn about Bhakti Yoga and to explore its practices and teachings. Furthermore, the rise of social media has made it possible for people to connect with others who are interested in Bhakti Yoga and to share their experiences and insights.

In modern India, Bhakti Yoga has become a popular form of spiritual practice, especially among the younger generations. Many young people are seeking a connection with their spiritual heritage and are drawn to Bhakti Yoga because of its emphasis on devotion and love. In addition, the practice of Bhakti Yoga has been embraced by people of all backgrounds and has been integrated into many different religious and spiritual traditions.

The contemporary resurgence of Bhakti Yoga has had a significant impact on modern India. This ancient spiritual tradition has gained a new following and is helping people to connect with their inner selves, find peace in their lives, and experience a deeper sense of connection with the divine. As Bhakti Yoga continues to grow in popularity, it is likely that it will play an increasingly important role in shaping India's spiritual legacy for generations to come.

"The Bhakti tradition, in its various forms
and expressions, has influenced spiritual
traditions around the world, including
Sufism, Christianity, and even contemporary
yoga practices."

IX

Music and Bhakti: The role of devotional music in Bhakti Yoga

Music has always been an integral part of Bhakti tradition in India, serving as a medium through which devotees express their devotion and love for the divine. From the hymns and devotional songs of the Bhakti saints to the modern kirtans and bhajans, music has played a vital role in the practice of Bhakti yoga.

The Bhakti saints, such as Kabir, Meera, Ravidas, and Tukaram, composed devotional songs and hymns in praise of the divine, offering their love and devotion through their music. These songs not only expressed their personal experiences with the divine, but also served as a way to connect with and inspire others on their own spiritual journeys. The use of music allowed the Bhakti saints to reach a wider audience, transcending linguistic and cultural boundaries and spreading their teachings across the Indian subcontinent.

In modern India, Bhakti yoga has experienced a resurgence in popularity, and devotional music continues to play a vital role in this resurgence. From traditional kirtans and bhajans to contemporary devotional music, Bhakti yoga continues to inspire and uplift people through the power of music. In modern Bhakti communities, devotional music is often performed in a group setting, providing an opportunity for devotees to come together in a shared experience of devotion.

The role of music in Bhakti yoga goes beyond just the expression of devotion, however. It is believed that the devotional music can bring the devotee into a state of meditation and spiritual absorption, helping to dissolve the ego and connect with the divine. The sounds of devotional music are said to have a profound effect on the mind and emotions, helping to purify the heart and bring peace to the soul.

The role of music in Bhakti yoga is an essential part of the tradition. It serves as a means of expressing devotion and connecting with the divine, and it continues to play a vital role in the practice of Bhakti yoga in modern India. Whether through traditional hymns and devotional songs or contemporary kirtans and bhajans, the power of music remains a powerful tool for spiritual transformation and connection with the divine in the Bhakti tradition.

ॐ

"In modern times, Bhakti yoga continues to be a source of inspiration and guidance for millions of people, offering a path towards inner peace and spiritual growth."

૪૭

X

Bhakti Yoga in everyday life: Practical applications of Bhakti Yoga in Modern Times

Bhakti Yoga, also known as the path of devotion, has been a central part of India's spiritual legacy for centuries. Bhakti Yoga emphasizes the importance of devotion to a personal deity or a Supreme Being as a means of attaining spiritual liberation. While Bhakti Yoga has been practiced for generations, it has never been more relevant or accessible than it is today. In this chapter, we will explore the practical applications of Bhakti Yoga in modern times and how this ancient spiritual tradition can be integrated into our daily lives.

The Importance of Devotion

At the heart of Bhakti Yoga is the concept of devotion. Devotion is the act of dedicating oneself fully to a particular deity, saint, or spiritual master. This dedication is expressed through various forms of worship, including prayer, ritual, and hymn singing. By practicing devotion, one can cultivate a deep and meaningful connection to the divine, which can lead to greater self-awareness and inner peace.

Incorporating Bhakti into Daily Life

One of the great benefits of Bhakti Yoga is that it can be incorporated into our daily lives in a variety of ways. For example, one can practice Bhakti Yoga by setting aside a specific time each day for prayer and meditation. This could be as simple as taking a few minutes to sit quietly and focus on the breath, or reciting a devotional hymn or prayer.

Another way to incorporate Bhakti into daily life is by participating in devotional activities, such as kirtan, or singing hymns in a group setting. This can be a powerful and uplifting experience, as the collective energy of the group helps to deepen one's connection to the divine.

In addition to these more formal practices, Bhakti can also be incorporated into our daily lives through acts of service and selflessness. By offering our time and resources to others, we can cultivate a deeper sense of compassion and love, which is a central tenet of Bhakti Yoga.

Bhakti Yoga offers a practical and accessible way for people to connect with the divine and cultivate a greater sense of inner peace and fulfillment. Whether through prayer, devotional activities, or acts of service, Bhakti Yoga can be integrated into our daily lives in a variety of ways. By embracing this ancient spiritual tradition, we can tap into the rich cultural and religious heritage of India and experience the transformative power of Bhakti Yoga for ourselves.

"Discovering India's spiritual legacy, and the significance of Bhakti yoga within it, is a journey of self-discovery and enlightenment."

৩

XI

The Global Impact of Bhakti Yoga: How Bhakti Yoga has influenced Spiritual Traditions Around the World

The Bhakti tradition, which originated in India, has had a profound impact on spirituality around the world. Bhakti yoga, which emphasizes devotion to a personal deity and the practice of devotion, has been embraced by people from diverse cultures and backgrounds. In this chapter, we will explore how Bhakti yoga has influenced spiritual traditions around the world and the ways in which it continues to shape spirituality in modern times.

One of the key aspects of Bhakti yoga is the focus on devotion to a personal deity. This devotion is expressed through various rituals and practices, such as singing devotional songs and hymns, performing puja (worship), and reciting prayers. This focus on devotion has had a significant impact on spiritual traditions in many cultures around the world.

One of the most notable examples of the impact of Bhakti yoga on spirituality around the world is the spread of devotional music. Bhakti yoga places a strong emphasis on devotional music, and this has influenced spiritual traditions in many cultures. For example, in Africa, devotional music has been used as a means of expressing devotion and as a way to connect with the divine. In Brazil, devotional music has played an important role in the growth of Afro-Brazilian religions, such as Candomblé and Umbanda.

Bhakti yoga has also influenced the spread of Hinduism outside of India. For example, the Bhakti movement has been instrumental in the growth of Hinduism in Southeast Asia, especially in Indonesia and Bali. In these regions, the Bhakti tradition has been integrated into local cultures, and the devotion to Hindu gods and goddesses has been expressed through music, dance, and other forms of art.

In addition to its influence on devotional music and the spread of Hinduism, Bhakti yoga has also had a significant impact on Sufism, the mystical tradition of Islam. Sufism is characterized by a focus on love and devotion to God, and many of its practices and beliefs are similar to those of Bhakti yoga. In fact, many Sufis have been inspired by Bhakti yoga, and the two traditions have had a significant impact on each other.

Bhakti yoga has also influenced the growth of other spiritual traditions around the world, such as Buddhism and Christianity. For example, in Japan, the Bhakti tradition has been integrated into the practice of Zen Buddhism, and in the West, Bhakti yoga has inspired the growth of devotional movements within Christianity, such as the Hesychast tradition in Eastern Orthodoxy.

The Bhakti tradition has had a profound impact on spirituality around the world. Its emphasis on devotion and the practice of devotional music have inspired the growth of spiritual traditions in many cultures, and it continues to shape spirituality in modern times. Whether through its influence on devotional music, the spread of Hinduism, or its impact on Sufism and other spiritual traditions, Bhakti yoga remains a powerful and influential spiritual practice.

"The study of Bhakti yoga and its role in
India's spiritual legacy offers a window into
the rich cultural and religious heritage of
India, providing a deeper understanding of
the country's history and spirituality."

଼ଓ

OTHER BOOKS OF THE AUTHOR

1. The Moments When I Met God
2. Kashiyile Theertha Pathangal
3. GURU GYAN VANI
4. Abhiprerak Gita
5. ASSI SE JAIN GHAT TAK
6. Hopelessness of Arjuna
7. The Soul and It's True Nature
8. Sense of Action (Karma)
9. Action through Wisdom
10. Action through Wisdom
11. THEORY AND PRACTICAL OF EVERY ACTION
12. LOGICAL UNDERSTANDING OF THE SUPREME
13. THE IMPERISHABLE SUPREME
14. Yatra Nishadraj se Hanuman Ghat Tak
15. Yatra Karnatak Ghat se Raja Ghat Tak
16. Yatra Pandey Ghat se Prayagraj Ghat Tak
17. Yatra Ranjendra Prasad Ghat se Dattatreya Ghat Tak
18. YaatraSindhiya Ghat se Gwaliar Ghat Tak
19. Yatra Mangala Gauri Ghat se Hanuman Gadhi Ghat Tak
20. Yatra Gaay Ghat Se Nishad Ghat Tak
21. MAA GANGA, GHATEN EVM UTSAV
22. Ganga Arti Dev Deepavali evam Any Utsav
23. Potentials of Digitalized India
24. VEDIC CONSCIOUSNESS
25. A Brief Introduction to Vedic Science
26. Kashi ke Barah Jyotirling
27. IMPACT OF MOTIVATION
28. Let's have a Milky Way Journey
29. Color Therapy in a Nutshell

30. Rigveda in a Nutshell
31. Yajurveda in a Nutshell
32. Samveda in a Nutshell
33. Atharva Veda in a Nutshell
34. Ayushman Bhava - Ayurveda
35. Srimad Bhagavad Gita and Upanishad Connection
36. Srimad Bhagavad Gita - an attempt to summarize each chapter.
37. Facts and Impact of Nakshatra
38. Astro Gems - NAVARATNA
39. Ekadashi - A Concise Overview
40. A Concise View of Hanuman Chalisa
41. Inspirational Gita
42. Nakshatraranyam
43. Summary of 18 Mahapuranas
44. Synopsis of 18 Upa Puranas
45. Rigvediya Upanishads
46. Shukla Yajurvediya Upanishads
47. Krishna Yajurvediya Upanishads
48. Samavediya Upanishads
49. Atharvavediya Upanishads
50. The Seven Great Sages
51. From Rocket Scientist to President Dr. APJ Abdul Kalam
52. The Visionary's Voice - Quotes of Dr. APJ Abdul Kalam
53. The Wisdom of Swami Vivekananda: Insights and Inspiration from a Legendary Spiritual Teacher
54. Ayurvedic Remedies from the Garden
55. Sages and Seers
56. Rising Strong – Motivational Stories of Women
57. Beyond Flames -Mystery stories of Funeral Ghat Manikarnika
58. The Origins of Tulsi: A Look at the Mythological Roots of the Plant"

59. The Holistic Cow: A Look at the Physical, Spiritual, and Cultural Importance of Cows in India
60. Arts of Healing
61. Exploring the Divine
62. Understanding Five Elements
63. The Etymology of Ram
64. Symbols of India
65. Voice of Change (About Speeches of Great Men)
66. She Speaks (About Speeches of Great Women)
67. Patriotism on Celluloid – Brief About Patriotic Films
68. The Music of Motivation: A Brief Guide to Inspirational Film Songs
69. **Unlocking the Secrets of the Dashopanishads**
70. A Cultural Mosaic
71. Ancient Traditions, Modern Minds
72. Ecos of Ancient Wisdom
73. Beneath the Surface
74. From Temples to Ashrams
75. Sages of the Subcontinent
76. The Art of Healling (Ayurveda, Yoga & Naturopathy)
77. Indian Kitchen
78. The Festivals of India
79. The Indian Epics Retold
80. The Power of Mantras
81. The Indian River Ganges
82. The Indian Architecture
83. Rites of Passage
84. The Indian Silk Road
85. The Indian Literature
86. The Indian Villages
87. The Indian Folks & Crafts
88. The Way of Buddha
89. The Ramayan of Tulsidas

CONTACT

DR. JAGADEESH PILLAI

MBA & PhD in Vedic Science

Four Times Guinness World Record Holder

Winner of Mahatma Gandhi Vishwa Shanti Puraskar and
Global Peace Ambassador

Gemology, Astro & Vastu Consultant - Spiritual Counselor

Consultant for designing World Record Ideas

Efficient Tarot Card Reader

9839093003

myrichindia@gmail.com

drjagadeeshpillai@facebook

drjagadeeshpillai@instagram
jagadeeshpillai@youtube

www. JAGADEESHPILLAI.com

|| LOKAHA SAMASTHAHA SUKHINO BHAVANTU ||

ॐ

www.ingramcontent.com/pod-product-compliance
Lightning Source LLC
Chambersburg PA
CBHW021120130726
47988CB00003B/1098